SONGS FROM GREEN PASTURES

Selections from the Psalms

Text: Good News Bible
© American Bible Society 1976

© Forlaget Scandinavia Copenhagen

First edition 1981
ISBN 87 87732 13 0

Printed by Toppan Printing, Singapore

SONGS FROM GREEN PASTURES

Selections from the Psalms

Edited by: Jørgen Vium Olesen

Forlaget Scandinavia Copenhagen

The Laws of the Lord

How clearly the sky reveals God's glory!
How plainly it shows what he has done!
Each day announces it to the following day;
each night repeats it to the next.
No speech or words are used, no sound is heard;
yet their voice goes out to all the world
and is heard to the ends of the earth.
God made a home in the sky for the sun;
it comes out in the morning like a happy bridegroom,
like an athlete eager to run a race.
It starts at one end of the sky
and goes across to the other.
Nothing can hide from its heat.
The law of the Lord is perfect; it gives new strength.
The commands of the Lord are trustworthy,
giving wisdom to those who lack it.
The laws of the Lord are right,
and those who obey them are happy.
The commands of the Lord are just
and give understanding to the mind.
The worship of the Lord is good;
it will continue for ever.
The judgements of the Lord are just;
they are always fair.
They are more desirable than the finest gold;
they are sweeter than the purest honey.
They give knowledge to me, your servant;
I am rewarded for obeying them.

No one can see his own errors;
deliver me, Lord, from hidden faults!
Keep me safe, also, from wilful sins;
don't let them rule over me.
Then I shall be perfect and free from the evil of sin.

May my words and my thoughts be acceptable to you,
O Lord, my refuge and my redeemer!

PSALM 20

We Trust in the Power of God

May the Lord answer you when you are in trouble!
May the God of Jacob protect you!
May he send you help from his Temple
and give you aid from Mount Zion.
May he accept all your offerings
and be pleased with all your sacrifices.
May he give you what you desire
and make all your plans succeed.
Then we will shout for joy over your victory
and celebrate your triumph by praising our God.
May the Lord answer all your requests.

Now I know that the Lord gives victory
to his chosen king;
he answers him from his holy heaven
and by his power gives him great victories.
Some trust in their war-chariots
and others in their horses,
but we trust in the power of the Lord our God.
Such people will stumble and fall,
but we will rise and stand firm.

Give victory to the king, O Lord;
answer us when we call.

God's Blessings

he king is glad, O Lord,
cause you gave him strength;
rejoices because you made him victorious.
ou have given him his heart's desire;
u have answered his request.

u came to him with great blessings
d set a crown of gold on his head.
asked for life, and you gave it,
long and lasting life.

s glory is great because of your help;
u have given him fame and majesty.
ur blessings are with him for ever
d your presence fills him with joy.

e king trusts in the Lord Almighty;
d because of the Lord's constant love
will always be secure.
e king will capture all his enemies;
will capture everyone who hates him.
will destroy them like a blazing fire
en he appears.

e Lord will devour them in his anger,
d fire will consume them.
ne of their descendants will survive;
king will kill them all.

ey make their plans, and plot against him,
t they will not succeed.
will shoot his arrows at them
d make them turn and run.

praise you, Lord, for your great strength!
will sing and praise your power.

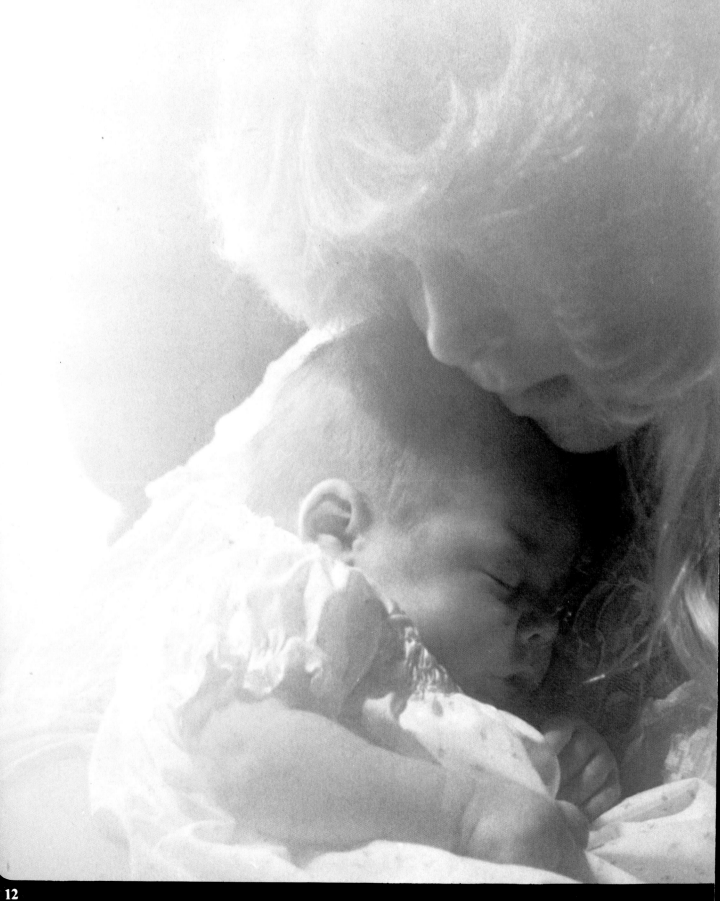

From PSALM 22

Stay Near to Me

My God, my God, why have you abandoned me?
I have cried desperately for help,
but still it does not come.
During the day I call to you, my God, but you
do not answer; I call at night, but get no rest.
But you are enthroned as the Holy One,
the one whom Israel praises.
Our ancestors put their trust in you;
they trusted you, and you saved them.
They called to you and escaped from danger;
they trusted in you and were not disappointed.

But I am no longer a man; I am a worm,
despised and scorned by everyone!
All who see me jeer at me; they stick out their tongues
and shake their heads. 'You relied on the Lord,'
they say. 'Why doesn't he save you? If the Lord
likes you, why doesn't he help you?'

It was you who brought me safely through birth,
and when I was a baby, you kept me safe.
I have relied on you since the day I was born,
and you have always been my God.
Do not stay away from me!
Trouble is near, and there is no one to help.
Many enemies surround me like bulls;
they are all round me,
like fierce bulls from the land of Bashan.
They open their mouths like lions,
roaring and tearing at me.

My strength is gone, gone like water spilt on the ground.
All my bones are out of joint;
my heart is like melted wax.
My throat is as dry as dust,
and my tongue sticks to the roof of my mouth.
You have left me for dead in the dust.

A Song of Praise

A gang of evil men is round me; like a pack of do[
they close in on me; they tear at my hands and fee
All my bones can be seen. My enemies look at me
and stare. They gamble for my clothes
and divide them among themselves.

O Lord, don't stay away from me! Come quickly
to my rescue! Save me from the sword; save my lif
from these dogs. Rescue me from these lions;
I am helpless before these wild bulls.

I will tell my people what you have done;
I will praise you in their assembly:
'Praise him, you servants of the Lord!
Honour him, you descendants of Jacob!
Worship him, you people of Israel!
He does not neglect the poor or ignore their sufferin
he does not turn away from them,
but answers when they call for help.'

In the full assembly I will praise you
for what you have done;
in the presence of those who worship you
I will offer the sacrifices I promised.
The poor will eat as much as they want;
those who come to the Lord will praise him.
May they prosper for ever!

All nations will remember the Lord.
From every part of the world they will turn to him
all races will worship him.
The Lord is king, and he rules the nations.

All proud men will bow down to him;
all mortal men will bow down before him.
Future generations will serve him;
men will speak of the Lord to the coming generatic
People not yet born will be told:
'The Lord saved his people.'

My Shepherd

The Lord is my shepherd; I have everything I need.
He lets me rest in fields of green grass
and leads me to quiet pools of fresh water.
He gives me new strength.
He guides me in the right paths, as he has promised.
Even if I go through the deepest darkness,
I will not be afraid, Lord, for you are with me.
Your shepherd's rod and staff protect me.

You prepare a banquet for me,
where all my enemies can see me;
you welcome me as an honoured guest
and fill my cup to the brim.
I know that your goodness and love
will be with me all my life;
and your house will be my home as long as I live.

The World Belongs to God

The world and all that is in it belong to the Lord;
the earth and all who live on it are his.
He built it on the deep waters beneath the earth
and laid its foundations in the ocean depths.

Who has the right to go up the Lord's hill?
Who may enter his holy Temple?
Those who are pure in act and in thought,
who do not worship idols or make false promises.
The Lord will bless them and save them;
God will declare them innocent.
Such are the people who come to God,
who come into the presence of the God of Jacob.

Fling wide the gates, open the ancient doors,
and the great king will come in.
Who is this great king?
He is the Lord, strong and mighty,
the Lord, victorious in battle.

Fling wide the gates, open the ancient doors,
and the great king will come in.
Who is this great king?
The triumphant Lord—he is the great king!

He guides me
in the right paths
as he has
promised.

Teach Me Your Ways

To you, O Lord, I offer my prayer;
in you, my God, I trust.
Save me from the shame of defeat;
don't let my enemies gloat over me!
Defeat does not come to those who trust in you,
but to those who are quick to rebel against you.

Teach me your ways, O Lord;
make them known to me.
Teach me to live according to your truth,
for you are my God, who saves me.
I always trust in you.

Remember, O Lord, your kindness and constant love
which you have shown from long ago.
Forgive the sins and errors of my youth.
In your constant love and goodness,
remember me, Lord!

I Come to You for Safety

Because the Lord is righteous and good,
he teaches sinners the path they should follow.
He leads the humble in the right way
and teaches them his will.
With faithfulness and love he leads
all who keep his covenant and obey his commands.

Keep your promise, Lord, and forgive my sins,
for they are many.
Those who obey the Lord
will learn from him the path they should follow.
They will always be prosperous,
and their children will possess the land.
The Lord is the friend of those who obey him
and he affirms his covenant with them.
I look to the Lord for help at all times,
and he rescues me from danger.
Turn to me, Lord, and be merciful to me,
because I am lonely and weak.
Relieve me of my worries
and save me from all my troubles.
Consider my distress and suffering
and forgive all my sins.

See how many enemies I have;
see how much they hate me.
Protect me and save me; keep me from defeat.
I come to you for safety.
May my goodness and honesty preserve me,
because I trust in you.

From all their troubles, O God,
save your people Israel!

Your Faithfulness Leads Me

Declare me innocent, O Lord,
because I do what is right and trust you completely.
Examine me and test me, Lord;
judge my desires and thoughts.
Your constant love is my guide;
your faithfulness always leads me.

I do not keep company with worthless people;
I have nothing to do with hypocrites.
I hate the company of evil men and avoid the wicked.

Lord, I wash my hands to show that I am innocent
and march in worship round your altar.
I sing a hymn of thanksgiving
and tell of all your wonderful deeds.

I love the house where you live, O Lord,
the place where your glory dwells.
Do not destroy me with the sinners;
spare me from the fate of murderers—
men who do evil all the time
and are always ready to take bribes.

As for me, I do what is right;
be merciful to me and save me!

I am safe from all dangers;
in the assembly of his people I praise the Lord.

Trust in the Lord

The Lord is my light and my salvation;
I will fear no one.
The Lord protects me from all danger;
I will never be afraid.
When evil men attack me and try to kill me,
they stumble and fall.
Even if a whole army surrounds me,
I will not be afraid;
even if enemies attack me, I will still trust God.

I have asked the Lord for one thing;
one thing only do I want:
to live in the Lord's house all my life,
to marvel there at his goodness,
and to ask for his guidance.
In times of trouble he will shelter me;
he will keep me safe in his Temple
and make me secure on a high rock.
So I will triumph over my enemies around me.
With shouts of joy I will offer sacrifices in his Temple;
I will sing, I will praise the Lord.

Hear me, Lord, when I call to you! Be merciful and
answer me! When you said, 'Come and worship me,'
I answered, 'I will come, Lord;
don't hide yourself from me!'

Don't be angry with me; don't turn your servant away.
You have been my help; don't leave me,
don't abandon me, O God, my saviour.
My father and mother may abandon me,
but the Lord will take care of me.

Teach me, Lord, what you want me to do,
and lead me along a safe path,
because I have many enemies.
Don't abandon me to my enemies,
who attack me with lies and threats.

I know that I will live to see the Lord's goodness
in this present life. Trust in the Lord.
Have faith, do not despair. Trust in the Lord.

A Prayer for Help

O Lord, my defender, I call to you.
Listen to my cry!
If you do not answer me,
I will be among those who go down
to the world of the dead.
Hear me when I cry to you for help,
when I lift my hands towards your holy Temple.
Do not condemn me with the wicked,
with those who do evil—
men whose words are friendly,
but who have hatred in their hearts.

Punish them for what they have done,
for the evil they have committed.
Punish them for all their deeds;
give them what they deserve!
They take no notice of what the Lord has done
or of what he has made;
so he will punish them and destroy them for ever.

Give praise to the Lord; he has heard my cry for help.
The Lord protects and defends me; I trust in him.
He gives me help and makes me glad;
I praise him with joyful songs.

The Lord protects his people;
he defends and saves his chosen king.
Save your people, Lord,
and bless those who are yours.
Be their shepherd, and take care of them for ever.

The Voice of the Lord

Praise the Lord, you heavenly beings;
praise his glory and power.
Praise the Lord's glorious name;
bow down before the Holy One when he appears.

The voice of the Lord is heard on the seas;
the glorious God thunders,
and his voice echoes over the ocean.
The voice of the Lord is heard
in all its might and majesty.

The voice of the Lord breaks the cedars,
even the cedars of Lebanon.
He makes the mountains of Lebanon jump like calves
and makes Mount Hermon leap like a young bull.

The voice of the Lord makes the lightning flash.
His voice makes the desert shake;
he shakes the desert of Kadesh.
The Lord's voice shakes the oaks
and strips the leaves from the trees
while everyone in his Temple shouts, 'Glory to God!'

The Lord rules over the deep waters;
he rules as king for ever.
The Lord gives strength to his people
and blesses them with peace.

Sing Praise

I praise you, Lord, because you have saved me
and kept my enemies from gloating over me.
I cried to you for help, O Lord my God,
and you healed me; you kept me from the grave.
I was on my way to the depths below,
but you restored my life.

Sing praise to the Lord, all his faithful people!
Remember what the Holy One has done,
and give him thanks!
His anger lasts only a moment,
his goodness for a lifetime.
Tears may flow in the night,
but joy comes in the morning.
I felt secure and said to myself,
'I will never be defeated.'
You were good to me, Lord;
you protected me like a mountain fortress.
But then you hid yourself from me, and I was afraid.

I called to you, Lord; I begged for your help:
'What will you gain from my death?
What profit from my going to the grave?
Are dead people able to praise you?
Can they proclaim your unfailing goodness?
Hear me, Lord, and be merciful! Help me, Lord!'

You have changed my sadness into a joyful dance;
you have taken away my sorrow
and surrounded me with joy.
So I will not be silent; I will sing praise to you.
Lord, you are my God, I will give you thanks for ever.

I will always
thank the Lord;
I will never stop
praising him.

A Prayer of Trust in God

I come to you, Lord, for protection;
never let me be defeated.
You are a righteous God; save me, I pray!
Hear me! Save me now!
Be my refuge to protect me; my defence to save me.

You are my refuge and defence;
guide me and lead me as you have promised.
Keep me safe from the trap that has been set for me;
shelter me from danger.
I place myself in your care.
You will save me, Lord; you are a faithful God.

You hate those who worship false gods,
but I trust in you.
I will be glad and rejoice
because of your constant love.
You see my suffering; you know my trouble.
You have not let my enemies capture me;
you have given me freedom to go where I wish.

Be merciful to me, Lord, for I am in trouble;
my eyes are tired from so much crying;
I am completely worn out.
I am exhausted by sorrow,
and weeping has shortened my life.
I am weak from all my troubles;
even my bones are wasting away.

All my enemies, and especially my neighbours,
treat me with contempt;
those who know me are afraid of me;
when they see me in the street, they run away.
Everyone has forgotten me, as though I were dead;
I am like something thrown away.
I hear many enemies whispering;
terror is all round me.
They are making plans against me, plotting to kill me.

From PSALM 31

In Your Care

But my trust is in you, O Lord; you are my God.
I am always in your care;
save me from my enemies,
from those who persecute me.
Look on your servant with kindness;
save me in your constant love.
I call to you, Lord; don't let me be disgraced.
May the wicked be disgraced;
may they go silently down to the world of the dead.
Silence those liars—all the proud and arrogant
who speak with contempt about righteous men.

How wonderful are the good things
you keep for those who honour you!
Everyone knows how good you are,
how securely you protect those who trust you.
You hide them in the safety of your presence
from the plots of men;
in a safe shelter you hide them
from the insults of their enemies.

Praise the Lord!
How wonderfully he showed his love for me
when I was surrounded and attacked!
I was afraid and thought
that he had driven me out of his presence.
But he heard my cry,
when I called to him for help.

Love the Lord, all his faithful people.
The Lord protects the faithful,
but punishes the proud as they deserve.
Be strong, be courageous,
all you that hope in the Lord.

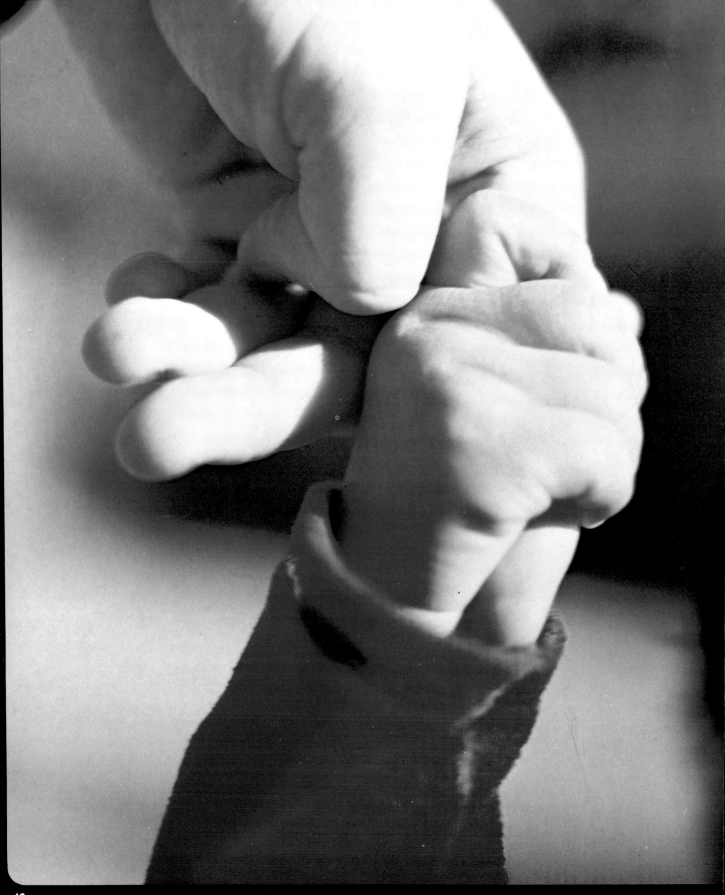

I Will Teach You

Happy are those whose sins are forgiven,
whose wrongs are pardoned.
Happy is the man whom the Lord
does not accuse of doing wrong
and who is free from all deceit.

When I did not confess my sins,
I was worn out from crying all day long.
Day and night you punished me, Lord;
my strength was completely drained,
as moisture is dried up by the summer heat.

Then I confessed my sins to you;
I did not conceal my wrongdoings.
I decided to confess them to you,
and you forgave all my sins.

So all your loyal people should pray to you
in times of need;
when a great flood of trouble comes rushing in,
it will not reach them.
You are my hiding place;
you will save me from trouble.
I sing aloud of your salvation,
because you protect me.

The Lord says, 'I will teach you the way
you should go; I will instruct you and advise you.
Don't be stupid like a horse or a mule,
which must be controlled with a bit and bridle
to make it submit.'

The wicked will have to suffer,
but those who trust in the Lord
are protected by his constant love.
You that are righteous, be glad and rejoice
because of what the Lord has done.
You that obey him, shout for joy!

From PSALM 33

Sing a New Song

All you that are righteous,
shout for joy for what the Lord has done;
praise him, all you that obey him.
Give thanks to the Lord with harps,
sing to him with stringed instruments.
Sing a new song to him,
play the harp with skill, and shout for joy!

The words of the Lord are true
and all his works are dependable.
The Lord loves what is righteous and just;
his constant love fills the earth.
The Lord created the heavens by his command,
the sun, moon, and stars by his spoken word.
He gathered all the seas into one place;
he shut up the ocean depths in storerooms.

Fear the Lord, all the earth!
Honour him, all peoples of the world!
When he spoke, the world was created;
at his command everything appeared.

The Lord frustrates the purposes of the nations;
he keeps them from carrying out their plans.
But his plans endure for ever;
his purposes last eternally.
Happy is the nation whose God is the Lord;
happy are the people he has chosen for his own!

The Lord Watches Over Those Who Obey Him

The Lord looks down from heaven
and sees all mankind.
From where he rules, he looks down
on all who live on earth.
He forms all their thoughts
and knows everything they do.

A king does not win because of his powerful army;
a soldier does not triumph because of his strength.
War-horses are useless for victory;
their great strength cannot save.

The Lord watches over those who obey him,
those who trust in his constant love.
He saves them from death;
he keeps them alive in times of famine.

We put our hope in the Lord;
he is our protector and our help.
We are glad because of him;
we trust in his holy name.

May your constant love be with us, Lord,
as we put our hope in you.

In Praise of God's Goodness

I will always thank the Lord;
I will never stop praising him.
I will praise him for what he has done;
may all who are oppressed listen and be glad!
Proclaim with me the Lord's greatness;
let us praise his name together!

I prayed to the Lord, and he answered me;
he freed me from all my fears.
The oppressed look to him and are glad;
they will never be disappointed.
The helpless call to him, and he answers;
he saves them from all their troubles.
His angel guards those who obey the Lord
and rescues them from danger.

Find out for yourself how good the Lord is.
Happy are those who find safety with him.
Obey the Lord, all his people;
those who obey him have all they need.
Even lions go hungry for lack of food,
but those who obey the Lord lack nothing good.

The Lord will Save His People

Come, my young friends, and listen to me,
and I will teach you to honour the Lord.
Would you like to enjoy life?
Do you want long life and happiness?
Then hold back from speaking evil
and from telling lies.
Turn away from evil and do good;
strive for peace with all your heart.

The Lord watches over the righteous
and listens to their cries;
but he opposes those who do evil,
so that when they die, they are soon forgotten.
The righteous call to the Lord, and he listens;
he rescues them from all their troubles.
The Lord is near to those who are discouraged;
he saves those who have lost all hope.

The good man suffers many troubles,
but the Lord saves him from them all;
the Lord preserves him completely;
not one of his bones is broken.
Evil will kill the wicked;
those who hate the righteous will be punished.

The Lord will save his people;
those who go to him for protection will be spared.

His anger lasts
only a moment,
his goodness for
a lifetime.

53

There is No One Like You

Oppose those who oppose me, Lord,
and fight those who fight against me!
Take your shield and armour and come to my rescue.
Lift up your spear and your axe
against those who pursue me.
Tell me you will save me.

May those who try to kill me
be defeated and disgraced!
May those who plot against me
be turned back and confused!
May they be like straw blown by the wind
as the angel of the Lord pursues them!
May their path be dark and slippery
while the angel of the Lord strikes them down!

Without any reason they laid a trap for me
and dug a deep hole to catch me.
But destruction will catch them before they know it;
they will be caught in their own trap
and fall to their destruction!

Then I will be glad because of the Lord;
I will be happy because he saved me.
With all my heart I will say to the Lord,
'There is no one like you.
You protect the weak from the strong,
the poor from the oppressor.'

Rescue Me

Evil men testify against me
and accuse me of crimes I know nothing about.
They pay me back evil for good,
and sink in despair.
But when they were sick, I dressed in mourning;
I deprived myself of food;
I prayed with my head bowed low,
as I would pray for a friend or a brother.
I went about bent over in mourning,
as one who mourns for his mother.

But when I was in trouble, they were all glad
and gathered round to mock me;
strangers beat me and kept striking me.
Like men who would mock a cripple,
they glared at me with hate.

How much longer, Lord, will you just look on?
Rescue me from their attacks;
save my life from these lions!
Then I will thank you in the assembly of your peop
I will praise you before them all.

ow Great is
e Lord!

n't let my enemies, those liars,
a over my defeat.
t those who hate me for no reason
rk with delight over my sorrow.

ey do not speak in a friendly way;
tead they invent all kinds of lies
ut peace-loving people.
ey accuse me, shouting, 'We saw what you did!'
ou, O Lord, have seen this.
don't be silent, Lord; don't keep yourself far away!
use yourself, O Lord, and defend me;
up, my God, and plead my cause.
re righteous, O Lord, so declare me innocent;
et my enemies gloat over me.
n't let them say to themselves,
e are rid of him! That's just what we wanted!'

y those who gloat over my suffering
completely defeated and confused;
those who claim to be better than I am
overed with shame and disgrace.

y those who want to see me acquitted
ut for joy and say again and again,
ow great is the Lord!
is pleased with the success of his servant.'
n I will proclaim your righteousness,
I will praise you all day long.

The Source of All Life

Sin speaks to the wicked man deep in his heart;
he rejects God and has no reverence for him.
Because he thinks so highly of himself,
he thinks that God will not discover
his sin and condemn it.
His speech is wicked and full of lies;
he no longer does what is wise and good.
He makes evil plans as he lies in bed;
nothing he does is good,
and he never rejects anything evil.

Lord, your constant love reaches the heavens;
your faithfulness extends to the skies.
Your righteousness is towering like the mountains;
your justice is like the depths of the sea.
Men and animals are in your care.

How precious, O God, is your constant love!
We find protection under the shadow of your wings.
We feast on the abundant food you provide;
you let us drink from the river of your goodness.
You are the source of all life,
and because of your light we see the light.

Continue to love those who know you
and to do good to those who are righteous.
Do not let proud men attack me
or wicked men make me run away.

See where evil men have fallen.
There they lie, unable to rise.

From PSALM 37

Trust in the Lord and Do Good

Don't be worried on account of the wicked;
don't be jealous of those who do wrong.
They will soon disappear like grass that dries up;
they will die like plants that wither.

Trust in the Lord and do good;
live in the land and be safe.
Seek your happiness in the Lord,
and he will give you your heart's desire.

Give yourself to the Lord;
trust in him, and he will help you;
he will make your righteousness shine
like the noonday sun.

Be patient and wait for the Lord to act;
don't be worried about those who prosper
or those who succeed in their evil plans.

Don't give in to worry or anger;
it only leads to trouble.
Those who trust in the Lord will possess the land,
but the wicked will be driven out.

Soon the wicked will disappear;
you may look for them, but you won't find them;
the humble will possess the land
and enjoy prosperity and peace.

The wicked man plots against the good man
and glares at him with hate.
But the Lord laughs at wicked men,
because he knows they will soon be destroyed.

The wicked draw their swords and bend their bow
to kill the poor and needy,
to slaughter those who do what is right;
but they will be killed by their own swords,
and their bows will be smashed.

The Lord Protects Those Who Please Him

The little that a good man owns
is worth more than the wealth of all the wicked,
because the Lord will take away
the strength of the wicked,
but protect those who are good.

The Lord takes care of those who obey him,
and the land will be theirs for ever.
They will not suffer when times are bad;
they will have enough in time of famine.
But the wicked will die;
the enemies of the Lord will vanish like wild flowers;
they will disappear like smoke.

The wicked man borrows and never pays back,
but the good man is generous with his gifts.
Those who are blessed by the Lord
will possess the land,
but those who are cursed by him will be driven out.

The Lord guides a man in the way he should go
and protects those who please him.
If they fall, they will not stay down,
because the Lord will help them up.

I am an old man now; I have lived a long time,
but I have never seen a good man
abandoned by the Lord
or his children begging for food.
At all times he gives freely and lends to others,
and his children are a blessing.

Put Your Hope in the Lord

Turn away from evil and do good,
and your descendants will always live in the land;
for the Lord loves what is right
and does not abandon his faithful people.
He protects them for ever,
but the descendants of the wicked will be driven out.
The righteous will possess the land
and live in it for ever.

A good man's words are wise, and he is always fair.
He keeps the law of his God in his heart
and never departs from it.

A wicked man watches a good man
and tries to kill him;
but the Lord will not abandon him
to his enemy's power
or let him be condemned when he is on trial.

Put your hope in the Lord and obey his commands;
he will honour you by giving you the land,
and you will see the wicked driven out.

I once knew a wicked man who was a tyrant;
he towered over everyone like a cedar of Lebanon;
but later I passed by, and he wasn't there;
I looked for him, but couldn't find him.

Notice the good man, observe the righteous man;
a peaceful man has descendants,
but sinners are completely destroyed,
and their descendants are wiped out.

The Lord saves righteous men
and protects them in times of trouble.
He helps them and rescues them;
he saves them from the wicked,
because they go to him for protection.

*The world
and all that is in it
belong to the Lord; the earth
and all who live on it
are his.*

The Prayer of a Suffering Man

O Lord, don't punish me in your anger!
You have wounded me with your arrows;
you have struck me down.

Because of your anger, I am in great pain;
my whole body is diseased because of my sins.
I am drowning in the flood of my sins;
they are a burden too heavy to bear.

Because I have been foolish, my sores stink and rot.
I am bowed down, I am crushed; I mourn all day long.
I am burning with fever and I am near to death.
I am worn out and utterly crushed;
my heart is troubled, and I groan with pain.

O Lord, you know what I long for;
you hear all my groans.
My heart is pounding, my strength is gone,
and my eyes have lost their brightness.
My friends and neighbours will not come near me,
because of my sores;
even my family keeps away from me.

From PSALM 38

My God Will Help Me

Those who want to kill me lay traps for me,
and those who want to hurt me threaten to ruin me;
they never stop plotting against me.

I am like a deaf man and cannot hear,
like a dumb man and cannot speak.
I am like a man who does not answer,
because he cannot hear.

But I trust in you, O Lord;
and you, O Lord my God, will answer me.
Don't let my enemies gloat over my distress;
don't let them boast about my downfall!
I am about to fall and am in constant pain.

I confess my sins; they fill me with anxiety.
My enemies are healthy and strong;
there are many who hate me for no reason.
Those who pay back evil for good
are against me because I try to do right.

Do not abandon me, O Lord;
do not stay away, my God!
Help me now, O Lord my saviour!

Hope in Suffering

I said, 'I will be careful what I do
and will not let my tongue make me sin;
I will not say anything while evil men are near.'
I kept quiet, not saying a word,
not even about anything good!
But my suffering only grew worse,
and I was overcome with anxiety.
The more I thought, the more troubled I became;
I could not keep from asking:
'Lord, how long will I live? When will I die?
Tell me how soon my life will end.'

How short you have made my life!
In your sight my lifetime seems nothing.
Indeed every living man is no more than
a puff of wind,
no more than a shadow.
All he does is for nothing;
he gathers wealth, but doesn't know who will get it

What, then, can I hope for, Lord?
I put my hope in you.
Save me from all my sins,
and don't let fools laugh at me.
I will keep quiet, I will not say a word,
for you are the one who made me suffer like this.
Don't punish me any more!
I am about to die from your blows.
You punish a man's sins by your rebukes,
and like a moth you destroy what he loves.
Indeed a man is no more than a puff of wind!

Hear my prayer, Lord, and listen to my cry;
come to my aid when I weep.
Like all my ancestors
I am only your guest for a little while.
Leave me alone so that I may have some happines
before I go away and am no more.

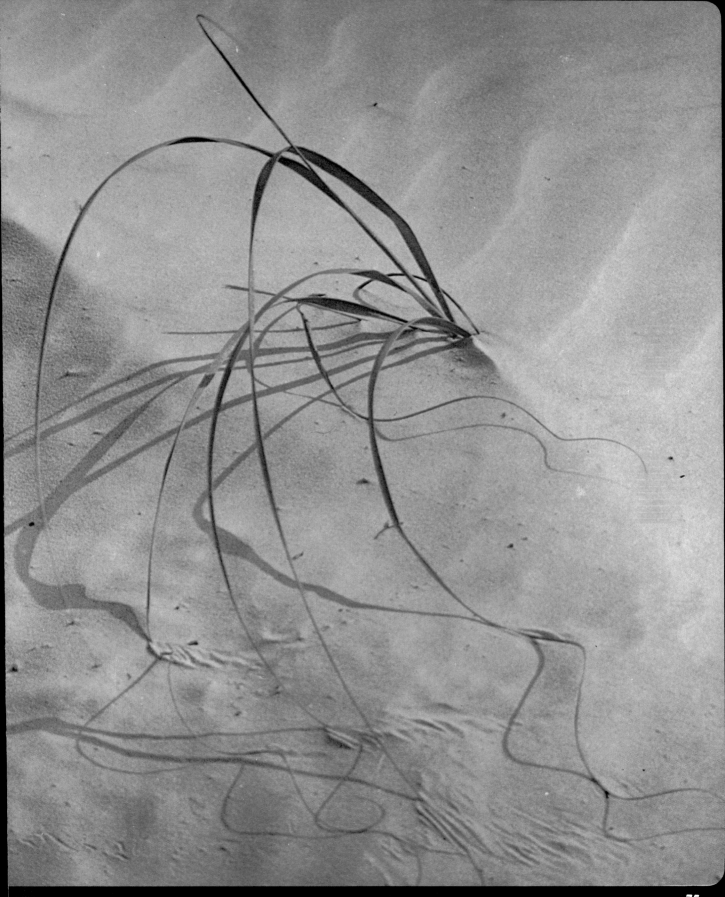

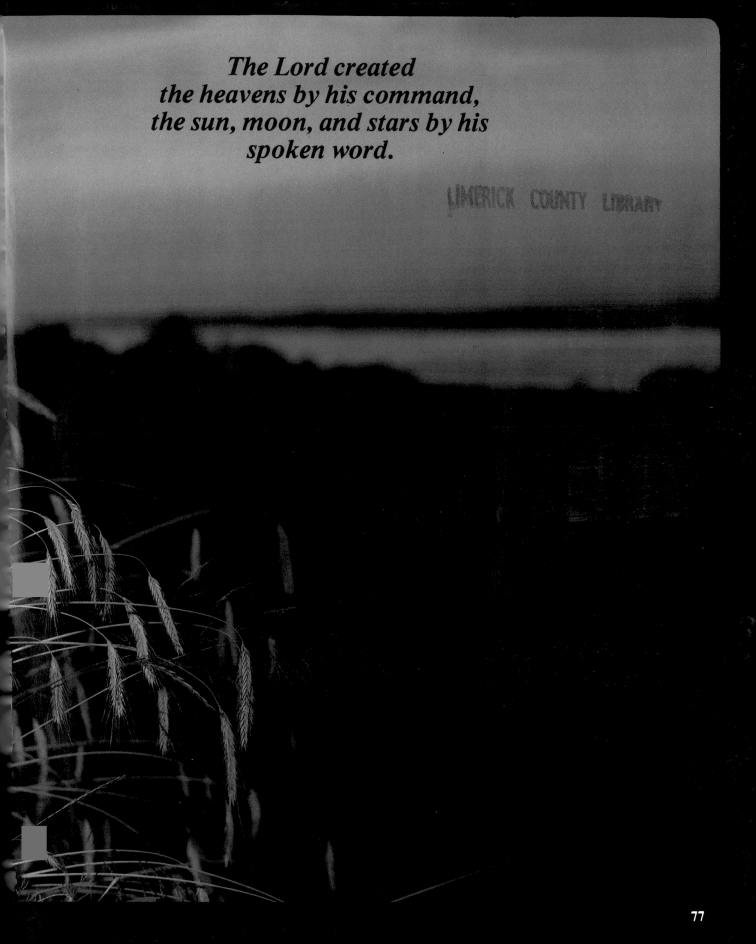

*The Lord created
the heavens by his command,
the sun, moon, and stars by his
spoken word.*